Lollipop Seeds

that Sprout for Kind Deeds®

An Easter Tradition

By Cherri Prince
Illustrated by Marco Bester

ISBN# 1-893013-11-7   www.lollipop-seeds.com   First Edition
Printed in USA

He lives
at the East Pole
where it always
is spring.

Jellybeans bloom
and chocolate birds
sing.

He has a **big** fluffy tail, and **long** floppy ears.

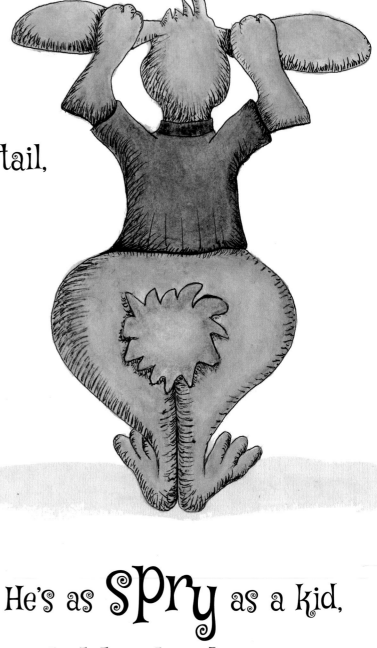

He's as **spry** as a kid, but has lived **hundreds** of years.

One day, he **hopped** by a squirrel,
who stops him and begs,
"**Why**, do you give out
candy and **eggs?**"

Easter Bunny laughed
and just **hopped** away.

What an obvious **question**

to take time from his day.

But later that day
he remembered his query.

And he thought and he thought
until he felt weary.

"I've delivered
the eggs and candy
so long...

I don't know WHY,
and that just seems
to be WRONG."

So, he checked
with his brothers
and they laughed
at his **question**

"Leave it alone," one shouted, "that's our suggestion."

Then he checked with his sisters who thought he was **Silly**.

"We do it for kids like **Violet, Frankie** and **Billy.**"

Then he checked with Grandma who's **wisest** of all.

"Grandma, why do I take on a task that's so **tall?**"

She sat for a moment, her eyes bright and **wide**,

while young Easter Bunny stayed close at her **side.**

THEN... she answered the best answer by far.

"The eggs stand
for hope that's born
on that **day**...

the candy for joy
that lights up your way.

And the **seeds**
that we give
to plant in the ground,

show us how love
blooms where
kindness is found."

Easter Bunny was quiet as can be.

"WHAT SEEDS?

No seeds have been delivered by me!"

"Oh dear,"

Grandma said, not believing her ears.

"How did I miss this for **all** of these years??"

"My sweet bunny boy, you've missed the best part...
These seeds from the East Pole are what grow a child's heart."

He still was
unsure of the value
of seeds...

especially for kids
who have
funner needs.

So, she went to a **box** by her necklace of beads...

And gave him instructions that go with the **seeds**.

Then, he curiously **reads**.....

Step One:

Do something **Kind**
for someone you know.

Step Two:

Make a wish for them too,
and the seeds
gently you'll t h r o w.

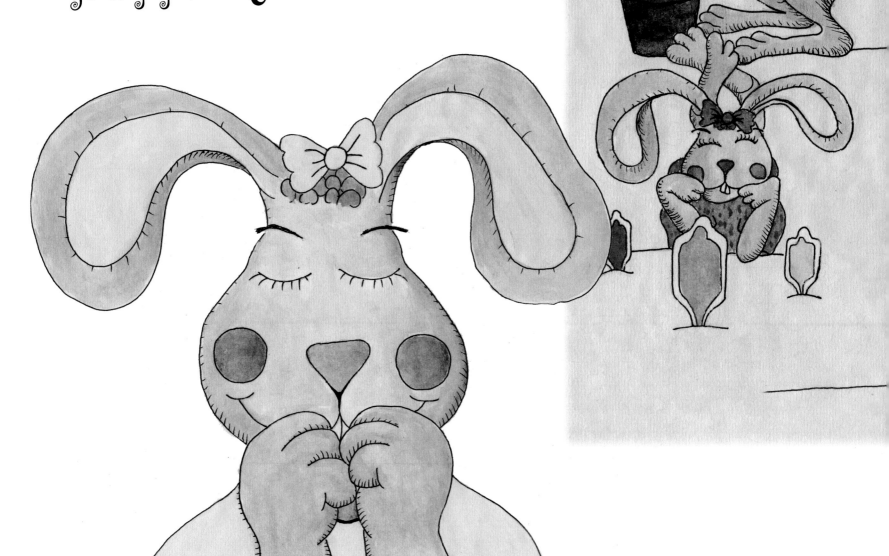